Series / Number 04-001

Comparing Elected and Appointed Judicial Systems

STUART S. NAGEL
University of Illinois

$) SAGE PUBLICATIONS / **Beverly Hills** / **London**

Copyright © 1973 by Sage Publications, Inc.

Printed in the United States of America

All rights reserved. No part of this book may be reproduced
or utilized in any form or by any means, electronic or mechanical,
including photocopying, recording, or by any
information storage and retrieval system, without permission in writing
from the publisher.

For information address:

SAGE PUBLICATIONS, INC.
275 South Beverly Drive
Beverly Hills, California 90212

SAGE PUBLICATIONS, INC.
St George's House / **44** Hatton Garden
London EC1N 8ER

International Standard Book Number 0-8039-0260-3

Library of Congress Catalog Card No. L.C. 73-80257

FIRST PRINTING

When citing a professional paper, please use the proper form. Remember to cite the correct Sage Professional Paper series title and include the paper number. One of the two following formats can be adapted (depending on the style manual used):

(1) NAGEL, S. S. (1973) Comparing Elected and Appointed Judicial Systems. Sage Professional Paper in American Politics 04-001. Beverly Hills and London: Sage Pubns.

OR

(2) Nagel, Stuart S., *Comparing Elected and Appointed Judicial Systems.* Beverly Hills and London: Sage Professional Paper in American Politics 04-001, 1973.

CONTENTS

I. Comparing the Judicial Behavior of Elected and
   Appointed Judges 7
II. Comparing the Selection Behavior of Judicial
    Voters and Appointers 17
        A. Voting Behavior in Judicial Elections 17
        B. Appointing Behavior in Judicial Appointments 23
III. Some Conclusions 36

Notes 40

References 43

Comparing Elected and Appointed Judicial Systems

STUART S. NAGEL
University of Illinois

There is abundant literature on the hotly debated topic of how American judges ought to be selected.[1] Indeed, it was part of the national high school debate topic in 1971 (Goldman, 1971). There has, however, been a lack of empirical data systematically comparing elected and appointed judges and the criteria by which they are chosen, with some exceptions.[2]

It is the purpose of this article to discuss some data that have been compiled and appropriate ways of gathering additional data in order to compare elected and appointed judicial systems. Comparisons might appropriately deal with (1) backgrounds and decisional propensities of elected judges and interim-appointed judges sitting on the same state supreme courts hearing the same cases, (2) the relative nonpartisanship and technical competence of various elected and appointed state supreme courts, (3) voting behavior of the electorate in judicial elections, and (4) appointing behavior of presidents and governors in judicial appointments.

Elected judicial systems in this context are those in which the judges are supposed to be initially voted into office by the general public in a special or general election, partisan or nonpartisan, with or without primaries. Appointed judicial systems are those in which all the judges are initially appointed by the governor, legislature, or combination of both,

---

AUTHOR'S NOTE: *This research is one of a series of policy science studies on measuring and achieving effects of alternative legal polities partly financed by the National Science Foundation, grant GS-2875. The NSF is not responsible for the results. The processing of the data for this article was mainly done at the Yale University Law School where the writer was a Russell Sage Fellow in Law and Social Science during 1970-71.*

TABLE 1
DIFFERENCES IN THE DECISIONS OF APPOINTED AND ELECTED JUDGES[a]

Type of Issue	% of Appointed Judges Above Their Court Average	Base of This % (apptd. judges)	% of Elected Judges Above Their Court Average	Base of This % (elected judges)	Difference Between the Percentages	Difference Just for Republican Judges	Difference Just for Democratic Judges
PUBLIC LAW							
Criminal Law							
1. For the defense in criminal cases	41	88	43	79	+2	+16	−6
Administrative Law							
2. For the administrative agency in business regulation cases	49	59	58	52	+1	+14	−10
Civil Liberties Law							
3. For finding a constitutional violation in criminal cases	41	32	47	34	+6	+22	+6
Tax Law							
4. For the government in tax cases	60	53	34	62	−26	−40	−15
PRIVATE LAW							
Family Law							
5. For the wife in divorce settlement cases	43	35	46	26	+3	+47	+6
Business Relations Law							
6. For the labor union in union-management cases	40	25	50	24	+10	+28	+13
7. For the consumer in sales-of-goods cases	38	32	56	41	+18	+14	+16
Personal Injury Law							
8. For the injured in motor vehicle accident cases	62	89	41	71	−21	−21	−20
9. For the employee in employee injury cases	41	71	49	65	+8	+8	+4

a. Using the nonunanimous decisions of the state supreme courts of 1955 on which both appointed and elected judges were present.

with or without provision for subsequent recall or approval-rejection elections.[3] Mention is made in the article where variations within the elected systems seem to produce differences in results, and likewise with variations within the appointed systems.

I. COMPARING THE JUDICIAL BEHAVIOR OF ELECTED AND APPOINTED JUDGES

DECISIONAL PROPENSITIES AND BACKGROUNDS

Elected judges are usually thought of as serving on different courts and hearing different cases from appointed judges. If that were always so, then any diverging characteristics between elected and appointed judges might be readily attributed to differences found between (1) the cases they hear, (2) the laws of the states in which they operate, or (3) the social, economic, and political climate of their respective states.[4] There are, however, many interim-appointed judges serving on state supreme courts along with elected judges—hearing exactly the same cases under the same legal rules within the same state social climate (Herndon, 1962). These interim-appointed judges fill out the unexpired terms of judges who die, resign, or retire.

Interim-appointed judges may not be the same as judges who never stand for election (since interim judges generally are voted upon in the next election subsequent to their interim appointments), but they do represent a form of judicial selection closer to appointment than the purely elected judge does. Whatever substantial differences are found between *interim*-appointed judges and elected judges can probably be extrapolated to be even greater between *fully* appointed judges and elected judges.

Table 1 shows how the decisional propensities of appointed judges differ from those of elected judges, using the nonunanimous decisions of the state supreme courts of 1955 on which both appointed and elected judges were present. "Appointed judges" here refers to judges on elected courts who were initially selected through an interim appointment, although they may have subsequently run for election. The most recent year for which these data and related data are conveniently available is 1955, but there is no reason to believe that appointed judges differed from elected judges any more or less in later years. Originally fifteen (rather than nine) types of cases were used, but six types of cases were eliminated because the number of appointed judges or elected judges for which nonunanimous cases were available was less than twenty.[5]

TABLE 2
HOW THE BACKGROUNDS AND ATTITUDES OF APPOINTED JUDGES DIFFER FROM THOSE OF ELECTED JUDGES[a]

Group 1 (Hypothesized to be more likely to be appointed)	Group 2 (Hypothesized to be more likely to be elected)	% of Appointed Judges in Group 2	Base of This % (apptd. judges)	% of Elected Judges in Group 2	Base of This % (elected judges)	Difference Between the Percentages	Difference Just for Republican Judges	Difference Just for Democratic Judges
I. GOOD DECISIONAL PREDICTORS								
1. Party Republicans	Democrats	27	37	50	40	+23	0	0
2. Religion Protestants	Catholics	19	37	39	23	+20	+51	−9
3. Liberal Attitudes Low general liberalism score	High general liberalism score	37	24	60	25	+23	+24	+17
II. GOOD VOTE-GETTING IMAGE								
4. Education Attended high-tuition law school	Attended low-tuition law school	74	35	54	39	−20	−38	−16
5. Years of Judicial Experience More than 17 years	17 years or less	52	21	36	11	−16	−27	−24
6. Scholarly Honors Honored as scholars	Did not so indicate	75	20	45	11	−30	−75	+29

a. Based on the state supreme courts of 1955 on which there was diversity on selection method and on the background differences.

General Liberalism

Hearing the same cases as their interim-appointed counterparts, elected judges tend to be on what might be considered the liberal side of nonunanimous cases in seven of the nine types of cases—although by only a small margin. Union versus management cases provide an illustrative example of the Table 1 findings. In these cases, 50% of the 24 elected judges (serving with interim-appointed judges) decided above the average of their respective courts for the union, whereas a lesser 40% of the 25 appointed judges decided above the average of their respective courts for the union.

One explanation that might be offered for why elected judges in general tend to be on the liberal side is that Democratic judges are more likely to be elected judges (given that Democrats tend to dominate the electorate—especially with relatively unknown judicial candidates), and Democratic judges are more likely to decide in favor of the liberal view (given the relatively liberal nature of the Democratic party). Thus, being elected and voting liberal might correlate because they are co-effects of being a Democrat. That this explanation is faulty, however, is indicated by the last two columns which show that if one compares only elected Republicans with appointed Republicans, or if one compares only elected Democrats with appointed Democrats, on the same courts, then the elected-appointed differences generally become stronger, not weaker. The elected-appointed differences show up much more when all the judges are Republicans than when all the judges are Democrats. This may be so because being a Republican—at least in the 1950s when these data were gathered—was a less unifying variable (among diversely selected judges on the same state supreme court) than was being a Democrat.

The explanation for the greater liberalism of elected judges possibly lies in the fact that elected judges may be more likely to be lawyers who have risen up from the political ranks and who have characteristics more like those of the general population or at least the more liberal elements in the general population. Appointed judges, on the other hand, may be more likely to be lawyers who formerly worked for top conservative law firms from which they were appointed to judgeships. This kind of explanation is partly confirmed in Table 2 which does show that elected judges are more likely to be Democrats, members of a minority religion, and more likely to have high liberalism attitude scores. Their background and attitude characteristics were determined by checking various "who's who" directories and by sending the supreme court judges a mailed attitude questionnaire.

The reason "political party" is held constant in the last two columns of Table 2 is to show that if one correlates a liberal background or attitude characteristic with being an elected rather than appointed judge, then the relation is not due to the intervening variable of party affiliation. For example, having a liberal attitude (L) may correlate with being a Democrat (D) rather than a Republican, and being a Democrat (D) may correlate with being an elected (E) rather than an appointed judge. Even so, having a liberal attitude (L) correlates with being an elected judge (E)—whether one makes this analysis with Republican judges only or with Democratic judges only. Likewise, most of the other findings in Table 2 are consistent, regardless of whether one uses all the judges, just the Republican judges, or just the Democratic judges.

Row 3 of Table 2 displays an interesting finding. It indicates (on courts which had some appointed and some elected judges and also some Protestants and some Catholics) that 39% of the elected judges were Catholics, and only 19% of the appointed judges were Catholics. This finding conflicts with the notion that "minorities have a better chance of placing their man by appointment than by election [because] governors are anxious to curry the favor of minority blocs and appointments are a very popular way to do it" (Winters and Allard, 1964). That notion does not adequately recognize that the judicial slatemakers of political parties where there are substantial minorities may be even more anxious to curry the favor of minority blocs.

Some Specific Types of Cases

Tax cases and motor vehicle accident cases did not follow the general pattern (shown in Table 1) of elected judges being more liberal. The explanation in tax cases might be that there is no clearly liberal position in tax cases unless one knows the type of tax (e.g., income or sales) or the type of taxpayer (e.g., corporate or consumer). Liberals do tend to favor the government in business regulation cases, but they disfavor the government in criminal cases, particularly where constitutional rights are involved. Some otherwise liberal judges have been known for their anti-government decisions in tax cases, such as Judge Musmanno of the elected Pennsylvania Supreme Court (Schubert, 1965: 150-154).

The explanation for motor vehicle accident cases may be more complicated. Like the tax cases, they may involve a mixture of issues as to both liability (on which liberals tend to find for the plaintiff) and damages (on which liberals sometimes do not think in dollar amounts as large as wealthy non-liberal types do, provided liability has been established). The personal injury cases may also be less ideological than the other types of cases and thus they may not distinguish liberal elected judges from conservative appointed ones as clearly as more divisive types of cases. The degree of divisiveness of the case can be determined by calculating the average percentage of dissents for each type of case or the average margin of victory for each type of case. Tax and personal injury decisions did not correlate as highly with party (Nagel, 1961b: 844), ethnic background (Nagel, 1962a: 98), or liberalism attitudes (Nagel, 1963: 40) as did business regulation, employee injury, criminal, or many other types of cases.

Perhaps another explanation for why elected judges were not so liberal in motor vehicle accident cases is indicated by one portion of Table 2. It appears that judges who are put up for election, rather than receiving an interim appointment from the governor, generally have good vote-getting images by way of having (1) attended a prestige law school (and thus come from wealthier backgrounds), (2) served many years in a prior judgeship (and thus are older judges), and (3) received scholarly recognition by way of publication[6] or membership in scholarly honorary organizations (and thus are more established). These characteristics are not consistently good general decisional predictors, as are party, religion, and liberalism; but they do happen to have a relatively high correlation with voting against the monetary claims of the injured party in motor vehicle accident cases.

It is possible that elected judges—given their education, judicial experience, and scholarly honors—tend to be more legalistic in deciding cases than appointed judges. This might cause them to have a greater propensity to reverse trial court decisions favoring the injured plaintiff in spite of the plaintiff's contributory negligence which legally bars him from recovering. This kind of trial court illegality is probably more likely to occur in motor vehicle accident cases than in the other types of cases.

Although the above explanations make some empirical sense, the deviant nature of the motor vehicle accident cases may be partly due to the chance presence of some untypical elected or appointed judges. The judges on the motor vehicle accident row are not the same set of judges as those on the other rows of Table 1, since the judges on a row depend on which judges or courts heard nonunanimous motor vehicle accident cases in the sample year among the total judges used. Although chance might explain one type of case, it is not so likely to explain seven or eight out of the nine, especially when one considers the size of the differences between the elected decisional propensities and the appointed decisional propensities (at least with Republican judges), and when one considers the size of the samples of the elected and appointed judges on which the percentages are based.

One finding in Table 1 possibly worth separate mention is the finding with regard to how elected judges differ from appointed judges in criminal cases. On the one hand, it might be argued that elected judges are more likely to favor the defense because elected judges tend to be more liberal in their decisional propensities, attitudes, and backgrounds. On the other hand, it might also be argued that elected judges are less likely to favor the defense because elected judges tend to be more sensitive to public opinion, and public opinion demands more convictions and severer sentences. Perhaps both these explanations balance each other and, as a result, Table 1 shows virtually no difference between elected and appointed judges in criminal case decisions.

Related to the above finding in criminal cases is the notion that although elected judges may be more liberal on economic matters than appointed judges (especially when one controls for political party), elected judges may be less liberal on civil liberties matters than appointed judges. This lack of civil libertarianism may be due to majoritarian public pressures to play down the rights of radical speakers and minority racial groups. In the sample of state supreme court judges, however, there were too few free speech cases or race relations cases to test this hypothesis, although elected judges were slightly more liberal in Table 1 on the constitutional rights of criminal suspects.

A related untested hypothesis is that judges with long terms of office (especially lifetime tenure) are more likely to decide in favor of broadening free speech and minority rights than are judges with short terms of office who are more subject to the majoritarian pressures of periodic elections. In data not shown in Table 1, judges with above average terms of office (over eight years) were slightly more liberal in handling the constitutional rights of criminal suspects, even though there is a strong negative relation between being elected and having a long term of office.

NONPARTISANSHIP

Just as the interim appointed judges were compared with elected judges with regard to their decisional propensities and backgrounds, so also comparisons could be made with regard to their nonpartisanship and technical competence. These two characteristics, however, tend to be more associated with courts rather than with judges. Thus, it makes more sense to talk of a court being nonpartisan by virtue of its balanced party representation than an individual judge being nonpartisan. Likewise, if the technical competence of a state supreme court is measured by the percentage of times it is upheld by the United States Supreme Court or favorably cited by other state supreme courts, then such a measure of competence accrues to the judges on that state supreme court collectively rather than to its individual judges.

For that reason, the methodology of within-court comparisons was not used in a related article by this writer dealing with the relative partisanship of elected and appointed judges (Nagel, 1961b: 848-850). The key data in that article (reproduced here on row 1 of Table 3) show that judges on appointed courts tend to be more nonpartisan than judges on elected courts in the sense that they were less likely to vote like typical Democrats or typical Republicans. A typical Democratic judge or an atypical Republican judge tended to vote in favor of the administrative agency in business regulation cases, the claimant in unemployment compensation cases, and the employee in employee injury cases. A typical Republican or an atypical Democrat tended to vote in the opposite direction in nonunaminous cases of these three types on courts having both Democratic and Republican judges present.[7]

Long term of office correlates positively with being appointed and positively with nonpartisanship. Long term, however, does not explain the positive correlation between being appointed and nonpartisanship, because the correlation remains when long-tenured appointed judges are compared with long-tenured elected judges on row 2. Likewise, appointed judges are not more successful in suppressing their values than elected judges, as is indicated on row 3 by the fact that appointed judges with liberal questionnaire attitudes tended to vote just as liberally as elected judges with liberal questionnaire attitudes.

Another possible explanation for the positive correlation between being appointed and nonpartisanship is the hypothesis that appointed judges are more atypical of their political party with regard to their attitudes than are elected judges because appointed judges must usually be nominated or approved by some bipartisan body and are sometimes appointed by governors across party lines. This explanation was tentatively discarded when it was found that appointed judges are just as likely to be conservative Democrats or liberal Republicans as elected judges are (as is shown on row 4).

Possibly the best explanation for the positive correlation (other than attributing it to chance in spite of the size of the correlation and the size of the sample) is that judges on appointed courts consciously or subconsciously view their roles as being more nonpartisan than do judges on elected courts. Unfortunately, none of the questionnaire or interviewing surveys of state judiciaries have specifically dealt with how individual judges perceive their relations with Democratic or Republican party

TABLE 3
SOME ASPECTS OF HOW ELECTED JUDGES DIFFER FROM APPOINTED JUDGES ON NONPARTISANSHIP AND TECHNICAL COMPETENCE

Group 1 (A quality often thought to be *less* desirable)	Group 2 (A quality often thought to be *more* desirable)	Number of Judges or Courts		% Elected in Group 1	% Appointed in Group 1	Difference Between Percentages
		Elected	Appointed			
I. NONPARTISANSHIP		(Judges on elected courts)	(Judges on appointed courts)			
1. Judges who voted in *accordance* with their party pattern	Judges who voted *contrary* to their party pattern	47	18	15%	39%	+24
2. Judges who voted in *accordance* with their party pattern	Judges who voted *contrary* to their party pattern	20	17	15	41	+26
3. Judges who voted in *accordance* with their value position	Judges who voted *contrary* to their value position in criminal cases	59 (all with over 8-year terms)	6	64	67	+3
4. Being a liberal Democrat or conservative Republican	Being a conservative Democrat or liberal Republican	17	8	50	53	−3
5. Having a *less* nonpartisan role perception	Having a *more* nonpartisan role perception	—	—	>50?	<50?	+?

TABLE 3 (Continued)

Group 1 (A quality often thought to be *less* desirable)	Group 2 (A quality often thought to be *more* desirable)	Number of Judges or Courts		% Elected in Group 1	% Appointed in Group 1	Difference Between Percentages
		Elected	Appointed			
II. TECHNICAL COMPETENCE		(elected courts)	(appointed courts)			
6. Courts having *below* average prestige	Courts having *above* average prestige	38	10	37%	40%	+3
7. Courts deciding *below* average number of cases per judge per year	Courts deciding *above* average number of cases per judge per year	31	11	42	18	−24
8. Courts *not* clearing their full annual docket	Courts clearing their full annual docket	30	9	57	89	+32

[15]

positions (as is indicated by the blanks and question marks on row 5). Appointed judges may have a more positive attitude toward judicial law-making rather than mere law-finding, but such a role perception does not necessarily relate to partisanship or nonpartisanship (Vines, 1969).

TECHNICAL COMPETENCE

One could measure the relative technical competence of elected and appointed state supreme courts by determining for each state supreme court (1) the esteem in which they are held by law professors through a mailed questionnaire, (2) the frequency with which their opinions are included in law school casebooks, and (3) the extent to which they are favorably cited by other courts. All three prestige-competence measures were used by Rodney Mott (1936) to rank the 48 state supreme courts during the 1930s. No more recent ranking has been prepared.

Row 6 of Table 3 shows that there is virtually no difference in the relative prestige of the elected and appointed state supreme courts using the Mott combined prestige ratings. The top five state supreme courts were New York, Massachusetts, Illinois, New Jersey, and California. At that time only Massachusetts and New Jersey were appointed courts, although California subsequently adopted an appointive system. There is likewise virtually no difference between elected and appointed courts if the components of the combined prestige index are used, since the components correlate so highly with the combined index and with each other.

Determining the prestige or competence of state supreme courts by looking to favorable mentions by law professors, casebooks, or other courts may, however, be more a reflection of the quantity of cases generated by the economy and society of the state than a reflection of the technical competence of the court. Likewise, the percentage of times a state supreme court is upheld by the United States Supreme Court (or favorably cited by law professors) may be more a measure of the ideological similarity between the two levels of courts, rather than a measure of technical competence.

A measure of technical competence that at least at first seems less subjective than using the ratings of law professors or other courts is to determine the relative ability of elected courts and appointed courts (1) to handle many cases per judge per year, or (2) to clear their full annual docket of appeals. The Institute of Judicial Administration in 1954 prepared a report entitled "Statistics on Work of Highest State Appellate Courts" which contains the latest available raw data in one place for making such a comparison.

Row 7 of Table 3 shows that a higher percentage of elected courts (42%) were below the national average with regard to the number of cases decided per judge for 1953, as contrasted to the appointed courts (18%). Row 8, however, shows that a lower percentage of elected courts (57%) failed to decide as many appeals in 1953 as had been argued or submitted as contrasted to the appointed courts (89%).

These two rows of comparisons, however, are not very meaningful in view of the fact that the different state supreme courts seem to have highly different notions of what constitutes a case. For instance, some include and some exclude certiorari denials in counting cases submitted and cases decided. Inconsistent definitions of what constitutes a case thus seem to explain why the elected supreme court of the state of Florida, for example, claims to have decided 991 cases in 1953 and the appointed court of New Jersey claims to have decided only 163.

There may be some value in using the ratings of law professors and other courts to determine the technical competence of state supreme courts provided that some statistical adjustments are made to control for the quantity of cases each court generates and the liberalism ideological factor. Likewise there may be some value in using case output and backlog statistics, provided there is a common definition of what constitutes a case. A more sophisticated measure of whether the decisions were "objectively correct" may, however, be impossible—especially when one is dealing with the kind of policy-oriented problems which exist at the state supreme court level. What is "objectively correct" may ultimately depend on one's liberal or conservative value position, which takes us back to comparing elected and appointed judges on their decisional propensities.

II. COMPARING THE SELECTION BEHAVIOR OF JUDICIAL VOTERS AND APPOINTERS
A. VOTING BEHAVIOR IN JUDICIAL ELECTIONS

In order to compare elected and appointed judicial systems, it makes sense not only to compare the judicial behavior of elected and appointed judges, but also to compare the selection behavior of judicial voters and appointers.[8]

VOTING TURNOUT

A charge that is frequently made in attacking the elected system is to point out how few voters participate in judicial elections (Winters and Allard, 1964: 140). This may be true when judicial elections are held separately from general elections. When judicial elections are held at the

TABLE 4
HOW VOTERS WHO PARTICIPATE IN JUDICIAL OR GENERAL ELECTIONS DIFFER FROM THOSE WHO DO NOT[a]

Group 1 (Hypothesized to be lower participants)	Group 2 (Hypothesized to be participants)	Number in Each Group (1)	(2)	% of Group 1 Voters Who Participate	% of Group 2 Voters Who Participate	Difference Between Percentages
I. JUDICIAL ELECTION VOTERS (of those voting in the general election)						
1. Democrats	Republicans	336	327	83%	83%	0
2. Female	Male	372	439	78	85	+7
3. Under 45	Over 45	406	405	79	84	+5
4. Over 250,000 population	Under 250,000 population	500	311	83	80	−3
5. Poor people	Not poor	176	609	76	84	+8
II. GENERAL ELECTION VOTERS (among citizens age 21 or older)						
1. Democrats	Republicans	554	436	61%	75%	+14
2. Female	Male	644	629	58	70	+12
3. Under 45	Over 45	651	622	63	66	+3
4. Over 250,000 population	Under 250,000 population	872	401	59	77	+18
5. Poor people	Not poor	364	855	50	72	+22

a. Using data from the 1954 New York state elections.

same time as general elections, however, the percentage of general election voters who also participate in the judicial elections tends to run about 80-90%. For example, in a poll conducted by Elmo Roper and Associates of voters in the combined New York state general and judicial election of November 1954, 82% of the general election voters also participated in the judicial election (Roper, 1954; Klots, 1955).[9] In a nationwide sample of 47 combined congressional and judicial elections from 1950 to 1962 on which data were available, over 90% of the congressional voters participated in the simultaneous judicial election.[10] The New York figure may have been less than 90% because the simultaneous judicial election involved an especially long separate ballot.

When those who attack judicial elections mention low voter participation, they are implying that those who do participate are not representative of the general population of those eligible to vote. Conversely, then, if the actual participants (regardless of how small the percentage) are a representative cross-section of the general population, then no harm is done by the low participation with regard to obtaining a representative cross-section sample.

Table 4 provides some information with regard to the extent to which judicial election participants differ from those who do not participate. The data in the table come from the same Roper poll previously mentioned. Line 1 indicates there is no difference between the percentage of Democrats who participated in the general and judicial election and the percentage of Republicans who participated in the general and judicial election. Likewise, the top half of Table 4 shows that the general-plus-judicial voters do not differ substantially from the just-general voters with regard to sex, age, urbanism, or even economic class.

On the other hand, those who participate in the general election do differ substantially from those who do not. Seventy-five percent of all those polled who identified themselves as Republicans indicated they voted in the election for governor which was held the same day as the judicial election, whereas only 61% of those who identified themselves as Democrats did so. Likewise, 70% of the males polled voted in the gubernatorial election, but only 61% of the females did. There were even sharper differences between those whom the Roper pollsters defined as poor people and those defined as not poor. There was also an 18 percentage-point difference between people living in smaller communities (who vote more) and people living in larger cities (who vote less).[11] A less sharp difference appears along the age line—over 45 and under 45—although age differences might be more apparent if the data were broken down into ten-year age categories.

Thus, it appears that those who participate in judicial elections are more representative of general voters than those who participate in general elections are representative of the general public. It also appears that judicial voters are no less representative of the general public than general voters are. In spite of the unrepresentativeness of general voters with respect to important background characteristics, it has not been seriously proposed that voting for governor should somehow be replaced with an appointive process. Instead, the emphasis has been on trying to increase voting turnout in general elections rather than abolishing them.

Voting turnout can be increased in judicial elections (at least close to the level of voting turnout in general elections) if judicial and general elections are held simultaneously, as previously indicated. It is sometimes argued, however, that judicial elections should be held at a separate time from general elections even though that might greatly reduce the judicial voting turnout. The argument is made that holding judicial elections at the same time as general elections increases the incidence of "irrational" voting on the basis of the political party affiliation of the judicial candidates. It is therefore appropriate to discuss the factors which judicial voters consider in judicial elections, according to available data.

FACTORS CONSIDERED IN VOTING

First, it should be pointed out that it may not be so irrational—in terms of maximizing the voter's interests—for him to consider party labels and even ethnic surname connotations in judicial voting. This may be so in view of previous data which this writer has compiled which show Democratic judges do differ substantially from Republican judges in their decisional propensities in many important types of cases (Nagel, 1961b).[12] For instance, in a sample of 60 state supreme court judges serving on bipartisan state supreme courts in 1955 and hearing nonunanimous business regulation cases, 68% of the 25 Democratic judges were above the average of their court in deciding for the administrative agency, whereas only 23% of the 35 Republican judges were above their court average. Similar, although smaller, differences divided the Democratic judges from the Republican judges with regard to voting for the defense in criminal cases, the tenant in landlord-tenant cases, the labor union in union-management cases, the consumer in sales-of-goods cases, the employee in employee injury cases, and what might be considered the liberal direction in various other cases.

Likewise, previous data also show Catholic and other minority-ethnic judges do differ from Protestant and other majority-ethnic judges in their decisional propensities in important types of cases (Nagel, 1962a).[13] The differences are generally not so great or so consistent as with party affiliation, but ethnic affiliation does bear some predictive relation to the decisional behavior of the judges being voted upon. For instance, in a sample of 57 state supreme court judges serving on state supreme courts in 1955 having both Catholic and Protestant judges present and hearing nonunanimous criminal cases, 56% of the 18 Catholic judges were above the average of their court in deciding for the defense, whereas only 31% of the 39 Protestant judges were above their court average. Similar differences divided Catholic judges from Protestant judges with regard to voting for the administrative agency in business regulation cases, the employee in employee injury cases, and voting for the liberal direction in various other cases. Related differences were also found between judges whose family names indicated exclusively British ancestry as contrasted to judges whose family names indicated at least partial non-British ancestry.

Even if it were not generally in conformity with the voter's interests to consider party label or ethnic connotations, it should be pointed out that party and ethnic voting may be as prevalent in general elections as in judicial elections. A high percentage of voters in general elections do vote on the basis of party label (Campbell et al., 1954: 88-111). Of those voters who indicated their source of information about judicial candidates (in the Roper poll of the 1954 New York judicial election), 39% said they just supported the party ticket, 21% mentioned a newspaper recommendation, 15% said they had consulted family and friends who are not lawyers, 7% said they had consulted family and friends who are lawyers or followed bar association recommendations, and 17% mentioned other sources.

A meaningful way to compare party voting in judicial and general elections would involve determining the Democratic percentage of the two-party vote in a state supreme court judicial election held at the same time or as close in time as possible to a congressional election.[14] This was done in a nationwide sample of 112 congressional districts for bipartisan congressional elections held in 1960. In those congressional districts dominated by the Democratic party,[15] one would expect the Democratic vote percentage in judicial elections to be greater than the Democratic vote percentage in the accompanying congressional election—if party label is indeed more important in judicial elections. Table 5, however, shows that of 34 congressional districts dominated by the Democrats for which information was available, in only one of the districts was the Democratic vote percentage greater in the judicial election than in the congressional election. Among the 74 usable congressional districts dominated by the Republicans, in 40 of them the Republican vote percentage in the judicial election was greater than in the congressional election; and in 34 of the districts, those two percentages were reversed.

TABLE 5
HOW VOTERS IN JUDICIAL ELECTIONS DIFFER FROM VOTERS IN GENERAL ELECTIONS WITH REGARD TO PARTY AND ETHNIC VOTING[a]

I. TESTING THE HYPOTHESIS THAT THE DOMINANT POLITICAL PARTY WILL RECEIVE A HIGHER PERCENTAGE OF VOTES IN JUDICIAL THAN IN CONGRESSIONAL ELECTIONS (where both elections are bipartisan)

	Dominant Party in the Congressional District	
	Republican	Democrat
% Dem. Vote in Judicial Election Greater than % Dem. Vote in Cong. Election	Hypo. Refuted 34 districts	Hypo. Confirmed 1 district
% Rep. Vote in Judicial Election Greater than % Rep. Vote in Cong. Election	Hypo. Confirmed 40 districts	Hypo. Refuted 27 districts

% Confirmed = 41/102 or 40%;
% Refuted = 61/102 or 60%

II. TESTING THE HYPOTHESIS THAT ANGLO-SAXON EITHNIC SURNAMES WILL RECEIVE A HIGHER PERCENTAGE OF VOTES IN JUDICIAL THAN IN CONGRESSIONAL ELECTIONS (where both elections are bi-ethnic)

	Anglo-Saxon Candidate is with Dominant Party in Which Election	
	Both Elections or Neither Election	Only in One of the Two Elections
% Anglo-Saxon Vote in Judicial Election Greater than % Anglo-Saxon Vote in Congressional Election	Hypo. Confirmed 9 districts	Hypo. Untestable 3 districts
% Anglo-Saxon Vote in Judicial Election Less than % Anglo-Saxon Vote in Congressional Election	Hypo. Refuted 6 districts	Hypo. Untestable 7 districts

% Confirmed = 9/15 or 60%;
% Refuted = 6/15 or 40%

a. General Hypothesis: The dominant party or ethnic group will receive a higher percentage of votes in judicial than in general elections.

This means that of the 102 usable congressional districts, only 40% confirm the hypothesis that the dominant political party will receive a higher percentage of the votes in judicial elections than in congressional elections, and 60% of the districts refuted the hypothesis. It may be that voters believe that it is less proper or meaningful to vote party label in judicial elections and therefore may be more likely to look to other criteria in making judicial choices. It may also be that the criteria voters use in choosing judges has less of a correlation with political party than the more ideological criteria they use in choosing congressmen.

On the other hand, ethnic voting may be more important in judicial than in congressional elections, even if party voting is not. To determine this, one needs a sample of paired judicial and congressional elections in which both elections involve a candidate with an Anglo-Saxon name running against one with a non-Anglo-Saxon name. To control for the advantage which a candidate has who is with the dominant party, the only districts in which the ethnic hypothesis is testable are those in which the Anglo-Saxon candidate is with the dominant party in both elections or in neither. The bottom half of Table 2 indicates there were 15 such districts available from within the larger sample of districts on which data were compiled. Sixty percent of those 15 districts confirm the hypothesis that the Anglo-Saxon vote percentage in the judicial election is greater than in the congressional election. This means that the ethnic split was generally greater in judicial elections. This phenomenon may be due to the need of judicial voters to resort to ethnic surname connotations where more personalized knowledge of the candidates is lacking, especially where there are nonpartisan ballots. It may also be due to the reluctance of voters to emphasize ethnic considerations in congressional elections where ethnic balance on the ticket is not considered as important as it is on a multiple-judge court.

B. APPOINTING BEHAVIOR IN JUDICIAL APPOINTMENTS

In discussing factors considered in judicial election voting, it was pointed out (1) that party and ethnic voting may not be so irrational, and (2) that party and ethnic voting may not be so much more prevalent in judicial than in congressional or general elections. It should also be pointed out that emphasis on party and ethnic considerations may not be so strong among voters as it is among governors and presidents in making judicial appointments, an hypothesis to which we now turn.[16]

APPOINTING IN ONE'S OWN IMAGE

Presidents and governors do strongly consider party affiliation in making judicial appointments, as indicated by the high percentage of appointments within party lines. For example, of 102 appointments to the United States Supreme Court from John Jay through William Rehnquist, there have been only nine appointments across party lines (Schubert, 1960: 37, 709-712).[17] Eight of the nine involved Republican presidents appointing a Democrat to the court, possibly in light of the fact that Democrats have generally constituted a numerical majority in America even when Republicans occupied the White House. Justice Burton, a card-playing friend of Harry Truman, was the only Republican appointed to the Court by a Democratic president.[18] During the period from 1860 to 1960, over 95% of the appointments to lower federal courts by Democratic presidents were Democrats, and almost 95% of the appointments by Republican presidents were Republicans (Miller, 1956).

State governors in making appointments to state supreme courts are somewhat more likely to appoint across party lines. Thus, only 8 of 36 presidents appointed across party lines; but in a sample of 19 state governors, 11 made at least one appointment across party lines. State governors make more such appointments because in some appointive states (like Missouri) they are required by law to do so (Council of State Governments, 1955: Table 4); and in some elective states they possibly feel an obligation to occasionally replace a retired, deceased, or resigned judge by a member of the same party. Although presidents and governors may choose within party lines more so than voters do, presidents and governors supplement party information with personalized data which voters often lack.

Appointments across ethnic lines have been slightly more rare than appointments across party lines. Thirty-five of the 36 presidents through Richard Nixon have been Protestants. Only 7 of the Protestant presidents have appointed either a Catholic or a Jew to the Supreme Court, as contrasted to 8 who made appointments across party lines. The one non-Protestant president (John Kennedy) did name a non-Protestant (Arthur Goldberg) as one of his 2 appointments to the Supreme Court.

In the sample of 19 state governors, 16 were Protestants, 2 Catholic, and 1 unknown. Nine of the 16 never appointed a Catholic or Jew, although 7 of the 16 appointed at least 1 Catholic or Jew. The 2 Catholic governors both appointed at least 1 Catholic or Jew. The reason for fewer appointments along religious lines than along party lines may relate to the greater visibility, feeling of need, and the presence of legal requirements for bipartisan supreme courts but not for bi-ethnic supreme courts. Using a national sample of state supreme courts, political parties are much better represented in comparison to the general population than are the diverse American ethnic groups (Nagel, 1962a; 1961b).

By appointing judges like themselves, the presidents and governors not only promote their ideological causes and satisfy party patronage rewards, but they may also possibly receive subsequent judicial decisions favorable to the appointer. For example, in the case testing the constitutionality of President Truman's seizure of the steel mills during the Korean War, 50% of his appointees voted in favor of Truman, whereas only 20% of the Roosevelt holdovers voted in Truman's favor.[19] This case is consistent with the hypothesis that a greater proportion of judges appointed by the president are likely to vote for him than are the judges not appointed by the president.[20]

In a sample of 100 famous supreme court cases involving presidential power (as shown in Table 6), 23 confirmed the above hypothesis and 11 refuted it.[21] Forty cases neither refuted nor confirmed the hypothesis because the percentage of the President's appointees favoring him equalled the percentage of the President's non-appointees favoring him—which happens when the cases are unanimous, or when there is a zero correlation between being the President's appointee and voting in favor of him. Twenty-six of the cases were unusable because they did not contain some judges who were the President's appointees and some who were not. Since 23 cases confirmed and only 11 refuted, this amounts to 68% confirmation.[22]

Likewise, there is substantial confirmation of the hypothesis on row 2 of Table 6 that a greater proportion of the judges from the president's party are likely to decide for him than are the judges from the opposition party. Sixty-four percent of the usable, non-zero correlation cases confirmed the hypothesis.

For a president to appoint a former governor or president to the Supreme Court is also a form of appointing someone like oneself. Although there were only 19 non-zero correlation cases in which some former governors or presidents were involved, 12 of these 19 indicated a greater proportion of those former chief-executive judges voting for the president. However, merely having been a former governmental administrator does not seem to be a strong enough impetus for a judge to empathize with the president. This is indicated by row 4, where there were more refutations than confirmations of the hypothesis that a greater proportion of the judges who had been governmental administrators are likely to vote for the president.

TABLE 6
HOW VICTORY FOR THE APPOINTER RELATES TO WHAT JUDGES HE APPOINTS[a]

Hypothesis	No. of Cases *Not* Having Both Groups Being Compared (thus unusuable)	No. of Cases Refuting Hypothesis	No. of Cases Neither Refuting Nor Confirming Unanimous or Zero Correlation Cases	No. of Cases Confirming Hypothesis	% Cases Confirming Rather Than Refuting
1. A greater proportion of the judges *appointed by the president* are likely to vote for him (than are the judges not appointed by the president).	26	11	40	23	68%
2. A greater proportion of the judges *from the president's party* are likely to vote for him (than are the judges from the opposite party).	7	13	57	23	64%
3. A greater proportion of the judges who *had been governors or presidents* are likely to vote for the president (than are judges without such experience).	56	7	25	12	68%
4. A greater proportion of the judges who *had been governmental administrators* are likely to vote for the president.	0	23	62	15	39%

a. Using 100 famous Supreme Court cases involving presidential power.

OTHER FACTORS CONSIDERED IN APPOINTING

Although appointing in one's own image may be a very important factor in judicial appointments, other factors may also be important as well as interesting to discuss. These other factors include a desire to appoint judges who (1) will later be acclaimed for their judicial greatness, (2) will be approved by the legislature, (3) are young and will thus carry the appointer's ideology in the court for many years, and (4) possibly have had prior judicial experience. It may be interesting to try to determine what types of governors or presidents are most likely to appoint great, approved, young, or experienced judges, as well as judges across party or religious lines.

Table 7 shows the correlation between various appointer characteristics and various characteristics of judicial appointees where the appointee characteristics are often considered praiseworthy. The data for Table 7 come from analyzing the characteristics of 34 presidents through President Kennedy and the characteristics of the supreme court judges they appointed (Congressional Quarterly Service, 1963: 65-68). Table 7 also includes data on 16 governors and their appointed judges serving in 1955 in states where all the supreme court judges are appointed by the governor.[23] Information on the greatness of the judges who were appointed is available only for presidents and supreme court justices, using the lists of Felix Frankfurter (1957) and John Frank (1961: 43-44).[24] Likewise, information on whether some of the appointments were rejected by the legislature is also only readily available for presidents and supreme court justices.

The relationships that are particularly interesting to discuss are those involving a positive or inverse correlation between two of the variables that is greater than +20 or −20. For example, reading down each column of appointer characteristics, the first such substantial correlation is the +33 between being a governor rather than a president and making some appointments across party lines. This correlation may be due to the fact that some state laws which provide for appointive systems require the governor to provide some party balance on the supreme court, but nothing in the federal Constitution or statutes requires the president to do so. Governors are also more likely than presidents to appoint some supreme court judges who are Catholics or Jews rather than Protestants. This may be due to the lower visibility of appointments at the governor level than at the presidential level and to the fact that in some states Catholics and Jews comprise a much higher percentage of the population than they do in the nation as a whole.

TABLE 7
HOW APPOINTERS WHO MAKE GENERALLY PRAISEWORTHY APPOINTMENTS DIFFER FROM THOSE WHO DO NOT[a]

Appointee \ Appointer	Governor Not President	Former Lawyer	Former Legislator	College Educated	Republican Not Democrat	Opposition Controlled Legislature	Member Minority Religion
Some great judges	b	11	−04	01	−08	**48**	b
All accepted by legislature	b	**21**	**21**	−01	06	−10	12
Most had prior judicial experience	14	**22**	**22**	−07	**24**	19	−11
Some across party lines	**30**	10	−11	**28**	**29**	**23**	07
Some minority religion	18	−05	−16	13	−05	11	**35**

a. Decimal points preceding each correlation are not shown; boldface type indicates correlation greater than 20.
b. Information on this variable was available only for presidents or was otherwise limited.

Appointers who are former lawyers seem more capable of obtaining the consent of their legislatures to their appointments (+21)—possibly because of their greater negotiating ability and experience, but also because there is a substantial correlation between being a former lawyer and a former legislator since so many legislators are lawyers. Appointers who are former lawyers also tend to appoint more supreme court judges who have had prior judicial experience than non-lawyer appointers do (+26)—possibly because lawyers tend to think of supreme court judgeships as being more legalistic than non-lawyer appointers do. Like former lawyers, the former legislator tends to have his appointments more readily accepted by the legislature and tends to appoint persons with previous judicial experience. This may partially reflect the former legislator's greater awareness of how to win over the legislature.

"College-educated" in column 4 refers to having at least a bachelor's degree prior to 1900 or a graduate or professional degree after 1900. College-educated appointers tend to appoint more across party lines and to select more judges of minority religions. This might reflect the possible fact that better-educated appointers are more concerned with ability than with party loyalty or ethnic acceptability. Better-educated presidents, however, were no more likely to appoint great judges than less-educated presidents.

The most strictly political characteristics represented in the next two columns reveal some of the higher and more interesting correlations. Republican appointers, for instance, are more likely to appoint supreme court judges with prior judicial experience than are Democratic appointers. This may reflect their relative conservatism due to the increased age of appointees who have had prior judicial experience and the relative conservatism of Republican appointers. Republican appointers are also more likely to make appointments across party lines than are Democratic appointers. This conforms to the finding (not shown) that there is a +20 correlation between being a Republican appointer and having an opposition-controlled legislature, which may cause Republican appointers to feel a greater need to make more Democratic appointments than for Democratic appointers to feel the need to make Republican appointments. Republican appointers are more likely to have opposition-controlled legislatures because, for most of the time periods involved in the data, Democrats constituted a majority of the electorate although the electorate may have chosen a Republican as chief executive.

Having an opposition-controlled legislature produces the high correlation of +48 with appointment of some great judges. Apparently, appointers have a greater tendency or need to pick better qualified or at least more acceptable appointees if the appointer's party does not control the consent process in the legislature. This would also help to explain why appointers who have opposition-controlled legislatures tend to make more appointments across party lines and tend to appoint judges more likely to have prior judicial experience.

In the last row of the last column, once again we see the tendency of appointers, like voters, to favor their own image. Thus, there is a +35 correlation between an appointer being a member of a minority religion and his appointing some supreme court judges who are also members of a minority religion. As mentioned before, there has been only one president who was a non-Protestant (John Kennedy), and one of his two appointments to the supreme court was also a non-Protestant (namely, Arthur Goldberg). This same phenomenon of "like begets like" also appears in the governor appointment data.

BAR ASSOCIATION PREFERENCES

In order to more fully consider appointer behavior in judicial appointments, it might be helpful to determine what kinds of judges tend to receive high bar association endorsements. This is so because bar associations and lawyers seek to play important roles in the selection of judges in appointive systems by way of their membership on nominating commissions, as in Missouri, or by way of their membership on legislative approval committees, such as the U.S. Senate Judiciary Committee. Even in judicial elections, bar associations seek to exert an informal influence on determining the judges by way of their electoral endorsements.[25]

Table 8 shows how proposed federal judges who are rated relatively high by the ABA differ from those who are rated relatively low, using 270 appointees to the federal district and circuit courts from 1953 to 1962.[26] "Rated high" means they were declared to be exceptionally well qualified or well qualified. "Rated relatively low" means they were declared to be just qualified or unqualified before their appointment. The general hypothesis is that proposed judges having background characteristics more associated with liberalism will be rated lower than proposed judges having background characteristics more associated with conservatism. It is further hypothesized that higher ratings will go to judges having characteristics associated with technical competence and nonpartisanship. The general findings do not strongly support the liberalism hypothesis, but they provide more support for the technical competence and nonpartisanship hypotheses.

The top or liberalism half of Table 8 shows how political party, ethnic background, and bar association affiliations relate to the judicial ratings. Sixty-four percent of the 104 Democratic judges received high ratings, which is virtually equal to the 63% of the 153 Republican judges who received high ratings. It was thought that this equality might be due to high ratings being given to conservative southern Democratic judges offsetting the possible low ratings being given to liberal northern Democratic judges. However, there is still virtually no difference between the percentages when northern Democrats are compared with northern Republicans and when southern Democrats are compared with southern Republicans.

Likewise, American Bar Association preferences as manifested in their ratings do not significantly relate to whether the proposed judges are Catholic or Protestant. The ratings correlate more highly with whether the appointees have southern or eastern European ancestral nationality as contrasted to western or northern European ancestral nationality. There was also a 15 percentage-point difference between the percentage of foreign-born judges receiving high ratings and the percentage of native-born; but this difference could be attributable to the fact that there was only a small sample (8) of foreign-born judges.

The most relevant pressure groups in which potential judges are likely to be members are probably bar associations, since they take a stand (often conservative) on many issues that are involved in litigation (Schmidhauser, 1960: 65-99). Judges who indicated membership in the American Bar Association in *Who's Who in America* did not receive higher ratings than judges who did not indicate ABA membership. Judges who were ABA leaders, however, did tend to receive higher ratings than judges who were mere members. Membership in state and local bar associations did correlate more highly with the ratings, possibly because membership in these bar associations was more likely to be accompanied by leadership roles than membership in the far larger, more diluted ABA.

There are substantial correlations between the characteristics relating to nonpartisanship and receiving high ratings. For instance, those judges who had been less politically active received higher ratings than those who had been more politically active. To be classified as "politically active" meant holding elective political office, being a committeeman for either political party, or being a national convention delegate. Likewise, those proposed judges who had no prior legislative experience or no prior government executive experience also tended to receive higher ratings.

The characteristic related to technical competence that correlated most highly with ABA ratings was whether the proposed judge in his *Who's Who* biography listed any books or articles published. It does follow that one

TABLE 8
HOW PROPOSED JUDGES WHO ARE RATED RELATIVELY HIGH BY THE ABA DIFFER FROM THOSE WHO ARE RATED RELATIVELY LOW[a]

Group 1	Group 2	Number of Judges in Each Group (1)	(2)	% Group 1 Receiving High Rating	% Group 2 Receiving High Rating	Difference Between the Percentages
I. CONSERVATISM CHARACTERISTICS (less associated with conservatism)	(more associated with conservatism)					
A. POLITICAL PARTY						
1. Democrats	Republicans	107	153	64%	63%	−1
2. Northern Democrats	Northern Republicans	62	120	66	67	+1
3. Southern Democrats	Southern Republicans	45	33	61	63	+2
B. ETHNIC BACKGROUND						
4. Catholic	Protestant	40	126	60	62	+2
5. South or East Europe	West or North Europe	27	233	52	65	+13
6. Foreign born	Native born	8	245	50	65	+15
C. BAR ASSOCIATION AFFILIATIONS						
7. No ABA indicated	Indicated ABA membership	43	222	63	64	+1
8. No state bar indicated	Indicated state bar assoc. membership	50	209	52	66	+14
9. No local bar indicated	Indicated local bar assoc. membership	63	202	57	66	+9

TABLE 8 (Continued)

II. NONPARTISANSHIP AND TECHNICAL COMPETENCE (less associated with non-p. and tech. comp.)	(more associated with non-p. and tech. comp.)				
A. NONPARTISANSHIP					
10. More active in party	Less active in party	97	163	55%	68%	+13
11. Some legislative exp.	No legislative exp.	52	203	54	68	+14
12. Some govt. executive exp.	No govt. executive exp.	185	69	60	77	+17
B. TECHNICAL COMPETENCE					
13. No books or articles indicated	Books or articles published	186	84	59	74	+15
14. No academic experience indicated	Academic experience	198	45	66	60	−6
15. Little trial experience	Much trial experience	64	99	63	71	+8
16. No judicial experience	Some judicial experience	159	107	59	69	+10
III. MIXED CHARACTERISTICS (less associated with conservatism and maybe competence)	(more associated with conservatism and maybe competence)				
A. AGE					
17. Under 45	45 and over	70	135	56	64	+8
B. TYPE OF LAW PRACTICE					
18. Criminal, domestic or administrative	Corporate or financial	14	103	43	66	+23
19. Under five-man firm	Firm with five or more	150	103	56	73	+17

a. Using 270 appointees to the Federal Judiciary from 1953 to 1962.

who has published about law should be more technically competent to write judicial opinions and decide legal matters. Row 5, however, shows that the ABA preferred judges with no academic experience by six percentage points over those with academic experience. This may reflect the fact that academic experience correlates with a lack of practicing lawyer experience which the ABA considers more important, although academic experience might correlate with technical competence if all other things were held constant.

The most relevant practicing-lawyer experience is trial work, which does correlate with higher ratings. It makes sense that lawyers who have had extensive courtroom experience would make better judges. An even more relevant form of experience from the point of view of technical competence might be prior judicial experience. This characteristic also correlates with higher ratings. A more detailed breakdown of the "prior judicial experience" characteristic indicates that additional years of judicial experience go with higher ratings, if the lower judge is proposed for a higher federal judicial appointment. The preference of the ABA for judges with prior judicial experience in Table 8 is consistent with the preference of appointers who are former lawyers for judges with prior judicial experience in Table 7.

Prior judicial experience correlates with age as well as with ABA endorsement. Age possibly correlates with both increased technical competence and increased conservatism. Row 17 shows that older proposed judges are somewhat more likely to receive higher ratings than younger judges. This is especially so if one divides the judges by age into more than two intervals. Thus, 44% of those under 34 received high ratings, 57% of those between 35 and 44, 65% of those between 45 and 54, and 67% of those 55 and older. These figures include only district court judges because circuit court judges tend to be appointed at older ages and there are fewer of them.

"Type of clients" is another mixed characteristic that may correlate with conservatism and possibly technical competence such that it is hard to explain which of these two correlations accounts for the higher ratings which lawyers with a more prestigious type of clientele have over lawyers with a less prestigious clientele. Thus, row 19 contains the largest difference between the percentages; it shows that 66% of the 103 lawyers who had primarily corporate and financial clients received high ratings, whereas only 43% of the 14 lawyers who specialized in criminal, domestic, or administrative law practice received high ratings. The nature of the law practice of the proposed judges was mainly determined from consulting material in the Martindale-Hubbell *Legal Directory*. Related to type of clientele is "size of law firm." Lawyers from larger, more prestigious law firms did receive higher ratings possibly because of the presumed technical competence which large-firm members tend to have, but also possibly because large-firm members are likely to be bar association leaders. "Degree of urbanism" as a separate characteristic is not shown in the table because it correlates highly with size of law firm.

To supplement the above analysis of ABA ratings, one could determine the decisional propensities of the 270 appointees by analyzing their opinions to see if the judges with higher ABA ratings tend to be more conservative in business regulation and other types of cases which tend to separate conservative from liberal judges. In a study which had that as one of its purposes, no substantial decisional differences were found (Goldman, 1966). That study, however, did not compare high-rated federal judges with relatively low-rated judges hearing the same cases on the same three-judge districts courts or multiple-judge circuit courts in the way that elected judges were compared with interim-appointed judges in Part I of this paper. Therefore, the findings might be muddied by differences between the cases heard by high-rated judges and those heard by low-rated judges.

Likewise, one could try to get at the technical competence of the 270 appointees by doing a follow-up on their opinions—to see to what extent they were either upheld or cited favorably in subsequent cases. Appellate decisions were found for 147 of the district court appointees. Of 85 appointees who were highly rated, 33% were affirmed more than 80% of the time; whereas of 62 appointees who were not so highly rated, only 23% were affirmed more than 80% of the time. Likewise, using *Shepard's Citations* to determine how favorably or unfavorably the judge's opinions were treated by a subsequent court for 202 usable judges revealed that 20% of the highly rated appointees were favorably cited more than 40% of the time; whereas only 15% of the less highly rated appointees were favorably cited more than 40% of the time. Thirty-five percent of the less highly rated appointees were also unfavorably cited, but only 23% of the highly rated appointees were unfavorably cited.

Thus, it seems that bar association ratings, at least at the federal level, seem to correlate rather weakly with conservative background and decisional characteristics. They do correlate a little more strongly with background and decisional characteristics that relate to nonpartisanship and technical competence; but even there, their predictive power seems quite limited.

III. SOME CONCLUSIONS

Pulling together all the findings presented thus far leads one to conclude that elected and appointed judicial systems do not differ as much in their results or in the behavior of voters and appointers as the debate literature would have us believe.[27] It may, however, be more interesting to find little or no difference where a big difference was generally thought to exist or argued over than to have simply confirmed the conventional wisdom.[28] Nevertheless, some important differences between the two systems of judicial selection should be clarified.

COMPARING JUDICIAL BEHAVIOR

Elected judges serving on the same courts as interim-appointed judges do seem to be slightly more liberal in their decisions as, for example, in business relations cases involving consumers or unions. The liberalism differences show up especially when one only compares elected Republican judges with appointed Republican judges. Offsetting these liberalism differences, however, is the fact that the appointed judges were somewhat more likely to decide in favor of the injured party in less ideological motor vehicle accident cases, and judges with long tenure were more liberal in handling the constitutional rights of criminal suspects.

Likewise, elected judges serving on the same court as interim-appointed judges do seem to have (1) more liberal-predicting backgrounds with regard to political party and ethnic affiliation, and (2) more liberal off-the-bench questionnaire attitudes—even if political party is held constant. Offsetting that liberalism to some unknown degree is the possibility that elected judges are partly slated and elected for their greater vote-getting image, and they thus tend to have prestige law school degrees, years of judicial experience, and scholarly honors—all of which indicate a more conservative behavior pattern.

Judges on appointed courts were found to be more likely to vote contrary to the pattern of their political party than judges on elected courts, even when length of tenure was held constant. This finding, however, could not be explained in terms of greater attitudinal objectivity or having off-the-bench attitudes atypical of one's party, although it might possibly be explained in terms of differential role perceptions of appointed and elected judges.

There was virtually no difference between the elected and appointed courts on such measures of prestige or competence as the esteem in which they are held by law professors, the frequency their opinions are used in casebooks, or the extent to which they are cited favorably by other courts. Likewise, nothing meaningful could be concluded with regard to the ability of elected and appointed courts to process a large number of cases per judge or a large number of cases per cases submitted, mainly because of the inconsistencies among the courts as to what constitutes a "case."

COMPARING SELECTION BEHAVIOR

Two frequent charges made against elected judicial systems are that the voter turnout is so low in judicial elections as to make the elections meaningless; and that when the voters do vote, they do not do so in a meaningful way. On turnout, the data indicate that over 90% of the voters in general elections will vote in judicial elections if (1) the judicial elections are held at the same time as the general elections, and (2) the elections do not have an especially long ballot. The data also show those who vote in judicial elections are at least as representative of the general public as those who vote in general elections.

Voters in judicial elections may consider the political party and ethnic affiliation of the candidates when casting their votes. Empirical data, however, do tend to indicate that Democratic judges do differ in their decisional propensities from Republican judges, and that Catholic judges do differ from Protestant judges. The empirical data further show that voters in judicial elections consider party affiliations less than voters in general elections, although they seem more prone to consider ethnic affiliations.

On the appointive side of the picture, the appointments by presidents and governors strongly reflect political party and ethnic considerations. By appointing judges like themselves, presidents and governors not only promote their ideological causes and satisfy party patronage rewards, but the data indicate that they are thereby more likely to receive favorable decisions when their powers are involved in litigation before the court, especially if their appointees had been former presidents or governors themselves.

When one attempts to correlate a variety of characteristics of presidential and gubernatorial appointers with the characteristics of their judicial appointees, a number of findings are revealed. For example, former lawyer-legislators are more likely to appoint judges with prior judicial experience and are more likely to have their appointments accepted by the legislature. Presidents are more likely to appoint great justices to the supreme court when the opposition party controls Congress and approval is more difficult to obtain. Appointments across party lines are more likely to be made by governors than presidents, by better-educated appointers, by Republican appointers, and when the opposition party controls the legislature.

Bar associations often try to play an important part in judicial appointments at the presidential and gubernatorial levels, as well as in judicial elections. A systematic empirical analysis of what kind of judicial nominees get relatively high American Bar Association ratings shows that the ABA does not include a partisan political preference or a religious preference in its ratings. The ABA does tend to prefer (1) bar association leaders, although not mere members; (2) non-activism in partisan, legislative, or executive politics; (3) authorship and prior courtroom experience; and (4) lawyers in large firms engaged in corporate law practice. The ABA ratings correlate weakly with subsequent liberal-conservative decisional behavior of appointees, but a little more strongly with subsequent affirmation and favorable citation of appointees.

MAKING A POLICY CHOICE

From all these data, one should be in a better position to make an evaluative comparison between elected and appointed judicial systems, or at least to see better what further data are needed. In addition to empirical data, an evaluative comparison requires an awareness of what goals one considers desirable and possibly how much relative weight to give each goal. Thus if one values liberalism and public participation highly, but does not value so highly nonpartisanship and technical competence, then he may be more likely to prefer an elected system to an appointed system. Empirical data, however, can help inform one at least roughly how much or how little a difference in liberalism, public participation, nonpartisanship, or other variables there is between elected and appointed systems.[29]

If elected judges are more liberal than appointed judges (from the same political party on the same court) on economic matters, but less liberal on civil liberties matters as hypothesized, then it looks like a hopeless dilemma if one wishes to maximize or minimize both these ideological goals. One may, however, be able to maximize both by giving elected judges either lifetime or long tenure, as is done in Pennsylvania, where the supreme court judges are elected for 21-year terms. Likewise, one might be able to minimize both kinds of liberalism by appointing judges who must subsequently run for reelection against opposition or on their record. That is the situation in Missouri, where the supreme court is appointed, but stands for reelection every ten years; and at least one judge was defeated for his civil libertarian liberalism by a press campaign conducted by a conservative St. Louis newspaper.

Although the method of selection may correlate with a judge's economic background, and although term of office may relate to the amount of anti-civil liberties majoritarian pressure to which he is subjected, neither the method of selection nor the term of office seems to correlate very highly or consistently with technical competence, honesty, wisdom, and other non-ideological virtues. There was, however, some correlation in the data (1) between being *appointed* and deciding cases contrary to one's expected political party pattern; and (2) between being *elected* and attending a prestige law school, having years of judicial experience, and having received scholarly honors. What may be needed to supplement the provisions for method of selection and term of office is a non-ideological commission concerned with criteria, such as technical competence, honesty, and wisdom, in slating nominees for election or appointment and in removing judges who grossly fail to meet these standards.

Such a commission for nomination and removal proceedings could perhaps consist of five people: one judge, one law professor, one practicing lawyer, and two public representatives, or some other similar combination. The commission could be required to have no more than three persons from the same political party. They could be appointed by the governor with the consent of the legislature and with staggered terms, so that no one governor could appoint all the members at one time.[30] The judicial members could be appointed by the state supreme court and the lawyer members by the state bar association.

In the election process, two such commissions would be needed. One commission could aid the Democratic slatemakers and would be required to have the same occupational breakdown as the removal commission, but consist only of Democrats chosen at least partly in a Democratic primary. The other commission could aid the Republican slatemakers and be chosen at least partly in a Republican primary. These judicial election commissions (like the Missouri nominating commission) could by law have the power to require the slatemakers to choose judicial candidates from within the commission's recommended list or at least to choose a percentage of the candidates from the lists. This is analogous to the way the Democratic and Republican statewide slatemakers in Illinois rely on the Democratic alumni committee and the Republican alumni committee of the Alumni Association of the University of Illinois in slating candidates for the Illinois Board of Trustees.

Some of the above policy provisions (like those dealing with a possible

[40]

nominating commission to supplement the elected and appointed processes) go partially beyond the quantitative data presented, but all the above policy choices can obtain some insights and partial support from the figures. Equipped with a hierarchy of values and access to raw or analyzed data, policymakers in state conventions and legislatures should be able to make policy choices that will better achieve their goals on this controversial issue of elected versus appointed judicial systems.[31]

NOTES

1. Bibliographies include American Judicature Society (1970; 1967: 1-26), Dahl and Bolden (1968: 38-68), Klein (1963: 173-204), and Smith (1970).

2. Exceptions include Canon (1972), Henderson and Sinclair (1964), Jacob (1964), Levin (1972), and Watson and Downing (1969). Although these items contain some systematic quantitative data for comparing elected and appointed judges, they generally do not control for other important variables besides method of selection which might cause differences or similarities between the elected and appointed judges of different places. See note 4 below and the accompanying text.

3. See the annual editions of the *Book of the States* (Council of State Governments, since 1936) for the judicial selection methods that were used in each state since the 1930s.

4. These are the kinds of variables that are generally not controlled for in the quantitative comparative studies cited in note 2. This is particularly the case in Lee (1971) where he compares the liberalism of the decisional percentages of the four elected courts of Wisconsin, Ohio, Pennsylvania, and New York with the court percentages of the four appointed courts of California, Missouri, Massachusetts, and New Jersey. Levin (1972) only compares the decisions of the elected Pittsburgh judges with the appointed Minneapolis judges, but he does a depth analysis rather than just a statistical analysis.

5. Twenty was used as a cutoff partly to make theoretical sense out of the data presented and partly because Guilford says: "If one asks, How small is N before we have a small sample? . . . Some place it is as low as 20" (Guilford, 1956: 217). Guilford also advises that special statistics be used when any frequency is expected by chance to be less than ten (Guilford, 1956: 234-235). If the number of elected or appointed judges on a row is twenty or less, then by chance ten or less should be above their court average and ten or less should be below.

6. For further detail on the meaning of high-tuition law schools, see Nagel (1962b; 1969: 227). Herbert Jacob (1964) also found that elected trial court judges were generally more likely to have attended a prestige law school than appointed trial court judges, but both types of judges were about the same on law school honors and on having little prior judicial experience. For further detail on the meaning of years of judicial experience and scholarly honors, see Nagel (1963: 41-42).

7. As further support for the finding, when elected judges are compared with interim-appointed judges on the same courts with regard to deciding contrary to one's party pattern, a higher percentage of the appointed judges do make contrary

decisions than do the elected judges, especially among Republican judges. On the other hand, Francis Lee (1971) finds no significant difference between the appointed courts of California, Massachusetts, New Jersey, and Missouri on nonpartisanship as compared to the elected courts of New York, Pennsylvania, Ohio, and Wisconsin. He does not, however, use cases on which Democrats and Republicans are likely to differ, and he also uses sample sizes of one to four appointed courts compared with one to four elected courts, rather than many appointed judges compared with many elected judges.

8. Studies of voting behavior in a judicial election include Jacob (1966) and Ladinsky and Silver (1967), but they were not designed to compare judicial elections with general elections or judicial elections with executive appointments.

9. The writer gratefully thanks Phillip Hastings of the Roper Public Opinion Research Center at Williams College for the use of these data.

10. See the text accompanying Table 5 for further information on the source of the data.

11. If the area, however, gets small enough to be classified as "rural-farm," the voting turnout drops almost to the relatively low percentages of New York City and Buffalo.

12. Other works which found that Democratic judges differ from their Republican counterparts include: D. Leavitt (1972), Feeley (1971; 1969), Ulmer (1962), and Goldman (1966). No significant differences were found by Adamany (1969) and Walker (1972).

13. Other works which found that Catholic judges differ from their Protestant counterparts include Ulmer (1973; 1970) and Vines (1964: 353). No significant differences were found by Goldman (1966). Although Protestant judges seem to differ in their decisional propensities from Catholic judges, little difference is found on state supreme courts between British and non-British ancestral nationality as determined by surname connotation (Nagel, 1962a). There were, however, very few judges with paternal or maternal surnames that had a south Europe, east Europe, or other non-northwest Europe origin in the sample.

14. If judicial elections held simultaneously with general elections had a separate straight-party lever or box, then one could simply determine the percentage of straight-party judicial voters and compare it with the percentage of straight-party general election voters. There is, however, no separate straight-party indicator for judicial elections.

15. "Dominated by the Democratic party" here means that in the five congressional elections from 1952 through 1960, the Democratic candidate in the district won at least three times. If the Republican candidate won at least three times, then the district is considered to be Republican-dominated.

16. Studies of the process whereby presidents or governors appoint judges include: Chase (1972), Danelski (1964), Goldman (1967), Grossman (1965), Schmidhauser (1963: 183-232), Scigliano (1962: 65-97), and Watson and Downing (1969). With the exception of the Watson-Downing book, these studies are not, however, designed to compare the appointing process with the electing process.

17. The nine supreme court appointments across party lines were (1) Democrat Nelson who was appointed by Whig Tyler, (2) Democrat Field appointed by Republican Lincoln, (3) Democrat H. Jackson appointed by Republican Harrison, (4) Democrats Lurton and (5) J. Lamar appointed by Republican Taft, (6) Democrat Butler appointed by Harding, (7) Cardozo appointed by Hoover, (8) Burton

appointed by Truman, and (9) Brennan, who was an Eisenhower appointee. Brandeis, a Republican prior to 1912, is generally considered to have been a Democrat at the time he was appointed by Wilson.

18. Republican Justice Stone was also elevated from associate justice to chief justice by Democrat Roosevelt, and Democratic Justice White was elevated to chief justice by Republican Taft.

19. *Youngstown Sheet & Tube Company v. Sawyer* (1952). The two Truman appointees who voted against him said they would have voted in his favor if there had been danger of invasion (Burton), or if Congress had not passed a statute governing seizures (Clark).

20. For a discussion of whether presidents get what they want in the men they appoint to the supreme court, and a history of presidential litigation before the supreme court, see Scigliano (1971).

21. The 100 famous cases were found by drawing a sample from those listed in Corwin (1957) and Schubert (1957).

22. The writer gratefully thanks Gary Hoskin of SUNY at Buffalo for the work he did on compiling some of these data as part of a seminar paper.

23. The sixteen governors were: Adams of New Hampshire, Boggs of Delaware, Bradford of Massachusetts, Carvel of Delaware, Cross of Maine, Dale of New Hampshire, Donnelly of Missouri, Driscoll of New Jersey, Hildreth of Maine, Knight of California, Meyner of New Jersey, Marby of New Hampshire, Payne of Maine, Saltonstall of Massachusetts, Smith of Missouri, and Warren of California.

24. The sixteen justices who they both agreed had achieved greatness were Marshall, W. Johnson, Story, Taney, Curtis, Campbell, Miller, Field, Bradley, Harlan (the first Harlan), Brewer, Moody, Hughes, Holmes, Brandeis, and Cardozo. See also Nagel (1970).

25. However, less than 1% of the voters in the Roper poll (1954) mentioned bar association recommendations as being helpful in deciding which judge to vote for, even though bar association recommendations was one of five answers suggested by the pollsters. Bar association recommendations are more influential in the presidential appointment process. See Grossman (1965).

26. The writer gratefully thanks Linda Nielsen Metzler for her work in processing some of these data as part of her master's thesis (Metzler, 1965). Most of the raw data were generously provided by Joel Grossman of the University of Wisconsin.

27. For references to the debate literature, see note 1 above.

28. Examples include studies showing that: (1) the definition of criminal insanity may be irrelevant to outcomes in criminal cases; (2) the occurrence of equal apportionment may be irrelevant to legislative policy outcomes; or (3) the abolition of the principle of contributory negligence may be irrelevant to court congestion. See Dixon (1968: 574-581), Rosenberg (1959), and Simon (1967).

29. In writing this section, the writer benefited from a discussion with Donald Jackson, a former writer for Time-Life, Inc., who is preparing a forthcoming book on the American judiciary.

30. On the Missouri nominating commission, see Watson and Downing (1969). On removal commissions, see American Judicature Society (1965) and Braithwaite (1971).

31. On systematic legal-policy evaluation, see Mayo and Jones (1964) and Nagel (1966 and 1969: 360).

REFERENCES

ADAMANY, D. (1969) "The party variable in judges' voting: conceptual notes and a case study." Amer. Pol. Sci. Rev. 63 (March): 57-73.

American Judicature Society (1970) Judicial Selection and Tenure. Chicago: American Judicature Society.

--- (1967) Selected Readings on the Administration of Justice and Its Improvement. Chicago: American Judicature Society.

--- (1965) "Judicial misconduct." J. of the Amer. Judicature Society 48 (February): 163-195.

BRAITHWAITE, W. (1971) Who Judges the Judges: A Study of Procedures for Removal and Retirement. Chicago: American Bar Foundation.

CAMPBELL, A., G. GURIN, and W. MILLER (1954) The Voter Decides. Evanston, Ill.: Row, Peterson.

CANON, B. (1972) "The impact of formal selection processes on the characteristics of judges—reconsidered." Law and Society Rev. 6 (May): 579-594.

CHASE, H. (1972) Federal Judges: The Appointing Process. Minneapolis: Univ. of Minnesota Press.

Congressional Quarterly Service (1963) Current American Government. Washington, D.C.: Congressional Quarterly Service.

CORWIN, E. (1957) The President: Office and Powers. New York: New York Univ. Press.

Council of State Governments (1955) Courts of Last Resort of the Forty-Eight States. Chicago: Council of State Governments.

--- (since 1936) Book of the States. Chicago: Council of State Governments.

DAHL, R. and C. BOLDEN (1968) The American Judge—A Bibliography. Vienna, Virginia: Coiner.

DANELSKI, D. (1964) A Supreme Court Justice Is Appointed. New York: Random House.

DIXON, R. (1968) Democratic Representation: Reapportionment in Law and Politics. New York: Oxford Univ. Press.

FEELEY, M. (1971) "Another look at the 'party variable' in judicial decision-making: an analysis of the Michigan Supreme Court." Polity 4 (Fall): 91-104.

--- (1969) "Comparative analysis of decision-making on state supreme courts." Ph.D. dissertation. Minneapolis: University of Minnesota.

FRANK, J. (1961) Marble Palace: The Supreme Court in American Life. New York: Alfred A. Knopf.

FRANKFURTER, F. (1957) "The Supreme Court in the mirror of justices." Univ. of Pennsylvania Law Rev. 105 (April): 781-796.

GOLDMAN, S. (1971) "American judges: their selection, tenure, variety and quality." Current History 61 (July): 1-8.

--- (1967) "Judicial appointments to the United States Courts of Appeals." Wisconsin Law Rev. (Winter): 186-214.

--- (1966) "Voting behavior on the United States Courts of Appeals, 1961-1964." Amer. Pol. Sci. Rev. 60 (June): 374-383.

GROSSMAN, J. (1965) Lawyers and Judges—The ABA and the Politics of Judicial Selection. New York: John Wiley.

GUILFORD, J. (1956) Fundamental Statistics in Psychology and Education. New York: McGraw-Hill.

HENDERSON, B. and T. C. SINCLAIR (1964) Judicial Selection in Texas—An Exploratory Study. Houston: Univ. of Houston Public Affairs Research Center.

HERNDON, J. (1962) "Appointment as a means of initial accession to elective state courts of last resort." North Dakota Law Rev. 38 (January): 60-73.

Institute of Judicial Administration (1954) Statistics on Work of Highest State Appellate Courts. New York: Institute of Judicial Administration.

JACOB, H. (1966) "Judicial insulation—elections, direct participation, and public attention to the courts in Wisconsin." Wisconsin Law Rev. 1966 (Summer): 801-819.

——— (1964) "The effect of institutional differences in the recruitment process: the case if state hedges." J. of Public Law 13 (1): 104-119.

KLEIN, F. (1963) Judicial Administration and the Legal Profession—A Bibliography. New York: Oceana.

KLOTS, A. (1955) "The selection of judges and the short ballot." Record of the New York City Bar Assn. 10 (March): 103-113.

LADINSKY, J. and A. SILVER (1967) "Popular democracy and judicial independence: electorate and elite reactions to two Wisconsin Supreme Court elections." Wisconsin Law Rev. 1967 (Winter): 128-169.

LEAVITT, D. (1972) "Political party and class influences on the attitudes of justices of the Supreme Court in the twentieth century." Delivered at annual meeting of the Midwest Political Science Association.

LEE, F. (1971) "Judicial selection: an explanatory variable of judicial behavior on bipartisan state supreme courts." Ph.D. dissertation. Philadelphia: University of Pennsylvania.

LEVIN, M. (1972) "Urban politics and policy outcomes: the criminal courts," pp. 330-364 in G. Cole (ed.) Criminal Justice: Law and Politics. Belmont, Calif.: Duxbury.

MAYO, L. and E. JONES (1964) "Legal-policy decision process: alternative thinking and the predictive function." George Washington Law Rev. 33 (October): 318-456.

METZLER, L. (1965) "Characteristics of federal judges preferred by the American Bar Association." Master's thesis. Urbana: University of Illinois.

MILLER, B. (1956) "Politics and the courts; the struggle for good judges." Amer. Bar Assn. J. 42 (October): 939-978.

MOTT, R. (1936) "Judicial influence." Amer. Pol. Sci. Rev. 30 (April): 295-315.

NAGEL, S. (1970) "Characteristics of Supreme Court greatness." Amer. Bar Assn. J. 56 (October): 957-959.

——— (1969) The Legal Process from a Behavioral Perspective. Homewood: Dorsey Press.

——— (1966) "Optimizing legal policy." Univ. of Florida Law Rev. 18 (Spring): 577-590.

——— (1963) "Off-the-bench judicial attitudes," pp. 29-54 in G. Schubert (ed.) Judicial Decision-Making. New York: Free Press.

——— (1962a) "Ethnic affiliations and judicial propensities." J. of Politics 24 (February): 92-110.

——— (1962b) "Judicial backgrounds and criminal cases." J. of Crim. Law, Criminology, and Police Sci. 53 (September): 333-339.

――― (1961a) "Unequal party representation on the state supreme courts." J. of the Amer. Judicature Society 45 (August): 62-65.

――― (1961b) "Political party affiliation and judges' decisions." Amer. Pol. Sci. Rev. 55 (December): 843-850.

ROPER, E. (1954) "A study of voter awareness of judicial candidates in elections." (mimeo)

ROSENBERG, M. (1959) "Comparative negligence in Arkansas—a 'before and after' survey." Arkansas Law Rev. 13 (Spring): 89-112.

SCHMIDHAUSER, J. [ed.] (1963) Constitutional Law in the Political Process. Chicago: Rand McNally.

――― (1960) The Supreme Court—Its Politics, Personalities, and Procedures. New York: Holt, Rinehart & Winston.

SCHUBERT, G. (1965) The Judicial Mind—The Attitudes and Ideologies of Supreme Court Justices 1946-1963. Evanston, Ill.: Northwestern Univ. Press.

――― (1960) Constitutional Politics—The Political Behavior of Supreme Court Justices and the Constitutional Policies that They Make. New York: Holt, Rinehart & Winston.

――― (1957) The Presidency in the Courts. Minneapolis: Univ. of Minnesota Press.

SCIGLIANO, R. (1971) The Supreme Court and the Presidency. New York: Free Press.

――― [ed.] (1962) The Courts—A Reader in the Judicial Process. Boston: Little, Brown.

SIMON, R. (1967) The Jury and the Defense of Insanity. Boston: Little, Brown.

SMITH, S. (1970) "Bibliography: judges—appointment and removal—selected writings." New Haven: Yale Law Library. (unpublished)

ULMER, S. (1973) "Social background as an indicator to the votes of Supreme Court justices in criminal cases." Midwest J. of Pol. Sci. 17 (August).

――― (1970) "Dissent behavior and the social background of Supreme Court justices." J. of Politics 32 (August): 580-598.

――― (1962) "The political party variable in the Michigan Supreme Court." J. of Public Law 11 (Fall): 352-362.

VINES, K. (1969) "The judicial role in the American states," pp. 461-485 in J. Grossman and J. Tanenhaus (eds.) Frontiers of Judicial Research. New York: John Wiley.

――― (1964) "Federal district judges and race relations cases in the south." J. of Politics 26 (May): 337-357.

WALKER, T. (1972) "A note concerning partisan influences on trial-judge decision making." Law and Society Rev. 6 (May): 645-650.

WATSON, R. and R. DOWNING (1969) The Politics of the Bench and the Bar. New York: John Wiley.

WINTERS, G. and B. ALLARD (1964) "Two dozen misconceptions about judicial selection and tenure." J. of the Amer. Judicature Society 48 (December): 138-144.

Youngstown Sheet & Tube Company v. Sawyer (1952) 343 U.S. 579.

ADDENDUM to Section II-B: The writer thanks John Schmidhauser of the University of Iowa for supplying most of the data used for the U.S. Supreme Court judges. Basic data for the presidents come from C. Rossiter, **The American Presidency** (New American Library, 1956), pp. 161-162; the data on the governors, from the **Book of the States** (since 1936); data on the state supreme court judges—as elsewhere in this monograph—comes mainly from **Directory of American Judges** (American Directories, 1955).

STUART S. NAGEL is Professor of Political Science at the University of Illinois and a member of the Illinois bar. He is the author of The Legal Process from a Behavioral Perspective *(1969),* The Rights of the Accused *(1972), and the forthcoming* Improving the Legal Process: Effects of Alternatives, *as well as numerous journal articles. He has been a Yale Russell Sage Fellow in Law and Social Science and a Fellow of the Center for Advanced Study in the Behavioral Sciences. He has also been an attorney to the U.S. Senate Judiciary Committee, the Office of Economic Opportunity, and the National Labor Relations Board. He is the secretary-treasurer of the Policy Studies Organization and Coordinator of its* Policy Studies Journal. *In addition, he is a trustee of the Law and Society Association and a member of the editorial board of its* Law and Society Review.

E.T.S.U. AT TEXARKANA LIBRARY